Da'ath Magic for Beginners

Miracles: The Way to Extraordinary Magic

Contact: www.HarryEilenstein.de
Harry.Eilenstein@web.de
Harry Eilenstein at youtube

Production and publishing house: BoD – Books on Demand, Norderstedt

ISBN: 9783754312544

Table of Contents

I Da'ath Magic

"Da'ath" is a term from Kabbalah meaning "cognition, inner knowledge." "Da'ath" is the name of one of the eleven sephiroth (areas) on the Kabbalistic Tree of Life. This Tree of Life is a symmetrical structure consisting of approximately 40 elements. This structure is found in everything from vacuum cleaners and cars, to classical ballet and magic, to the German Constitution and nuclear physics – so it is a universal structure.

The most important characteristic of the area on the Tree of Life called "Da'ath" is the lack of boundaries – Da'ath is a continuum. Da'ath magic is consequently magic that takes place in a continuum, that is without boundaries – and that is therefore "extraordinary".

The counterpart to this is Yesod magic – Yesod on the Kabbalistic Tree of Life is the realm of life force, subconsciousness, dreams, etc. – in Yesod, like in Da'ath, everything is connected to everything else, but things are not boundary-less. Therefore, Yesod magic is not "extraordinary" but "ordinary".

Meaningful distinctions can be very helpful – this is true for all areas of life.

For example, in magic one can distinguish perceptual magic ("telepathy") from acting magic ("telekinesis") – the difference between these two aspects of magic is obvious.

A second form of distinction in magic is the distinction according to the goal: seeing the future, money magic, love spells, firewalking, storm spells, damage spells, healings, and so on. Again, everyone knows what is meant.

The distinction between Da'ath magic and Yesod magic is not so obvious at first – here the extent of magic is distinguished. This distinction makes sense, if one

a) can clearly distinguish the phenomena of the two types of magic

and/or

b) the two types of magic are performed in different ways

and/or

c) experiences these two types of magic fundamentally differently.

Ideally, all three forms of distinction apply.

The consideration of Da'ath magic (and also Yesod magic) has a real utility when it results in tangible instructions for Da'ath magic.

One could give different names to this form of magic:

- *"Da'ath magic"* – in reference to the sphere "Da'ath" on the Kabbalistic Tree of Life, which embodies the qualities of "delimitationless magic";

- *"Saturn Magic"* – in reference to the planet Saturn, which is associated with the Sephirah Da'ath;

- *"continuum magic"* – since Da'ath is a continuum;

- *"extraordinary magic"* – simply because it encompasses extraordinary phenomena;

- *"global magic"* – because it is boundaryless and therefore "global" (there is also a connection to globalization);

- *"magic of the collective subconsciousness"* – for Da'ath is, among others, the collective subconsciousness with the archetypes in contrast to Yesod, that is the individual subconsciousness with the images in an individual psyche;

- *"miracle"* – this would be the "classical term" for this kind of magic;

- Finally, there are some concepts which, although not identical with "Da'ath magic", are quite similar to it, such as the *"ice magic"* of Frater U.D. (even if we both do not agree in this – that both concepts are very similar …).

I 1. Phenomena

Of the three distinguishing criteria "phenomenon", "procedure" and "experience", the point "phenomenon" is the easiest to examine – even if this consideration will not be immediately precise.

The phenomena described in the following must of course be experienced by oneself to know that they really exist. If one has already experienced some of them, one can also accept the descriptions of similar phenomena that have been described to oneself by trustworthy persons.

- There are forms of magic where the only thing that matters is a realization. The most typical example of this is astrology, with the help of which one can, for example, describe the character of a person.

Here an analogy structure in the world is recognized (between the position of the planets and the character of a person).

- One step further is telepathy, by which one can receive information, which would be inaccessible in the normal way – e.g. recognize where someone has lost his front door key or what is in a package or what another, not present person is doing just now.

Here, information about spatially distant things is obtained in a non-physical, i.e. telepathic way.

- Also about information is the future vision, where one sees parts of the future.

Here information about temporally and maybe also spatially distant things is procured in a non-physical, i.e. telepathic way.

- In the many variants of wish-magic with the help of invocations, sigils, talismans etc. the "coincidence" is directed by the magician in an effective way according to his wishes.

Here the events are directed in a non-physical, i.e. telekinetic way.

The magical phenomena described so far have in common that they reveal an additional structure in the world which can be used by people: the analogies in astrology, the telepathic connections and the telekinetic guidance of "meaningful coincidence".

These forms of magic are first of all "only" an extension of the physical world view by a new kind of structure, connection and effect. At first there is no fundamental contradiction to the physical laws, because these magic phenomena can be combined with the natural laws to an extended world view, in which there are not only causal-scientific connections, but also magic-analogical connections.

- This changes, however, if one adds telekinesis phenomena like e.g. the simple experiment with the paper wheel on a needle point, which one can turn only by one's own will and one's own imagination. In this experiment one can prove a physical effect without physical cause – to describe this phenomenon a combinated causal-analogous world view is no longer sufficient.

You can watch this experiment at youtube e.g. under "psi-wheel" and then try it yourself. Nothing else is as convincing as one's own experience …

With some phenomena it is difficult to say what exactly happens with them. In such cases it is advisable to use the description which is the simplest and which can be explained with the fewest new assumptions.

- In a bilocation, a person appears in two places at the same time. However, there is another possible explanation than the duplication of the physical body.

It is known from hypnosis that one can suggest images to another person which that person then actually perceives. This can be carried so far that a person temporarily believes himself to be a dog, for example, and behaves like one.

Furthermore there are visions, i.e. inner pictures, which are combined with the optical perception of the outer world, so that the inner picture seems to be a part of the outer world. The unintentional version of this phenomenon is hallucination. These inner images, which one experiences as part of the outer world, can certainly speak and one can also touch them – they are therefore very difficult to recognize as an inner image.

Therefore, in the case of bilocation, the person who appears in several places at the same time could have sent his own image (consciously or unconsciously) to another place to cause something there.

Such bilocations are usually reported about saints, yogis, healers and similar "magic professionals".

Thus, a bilocation could be a vision willfully induced in another person.

- A similar borderline case is astral travel. In this case, one leaves one's own body with one's consciousness and with one's perceptive ability and can travel to any place, perceive and to a small extend also act there, and then return to one's body.

This can be described as a perfect form of telepathy if you like, but the experience of astral travel is still very impressive and does not feel like it is "just" advanced telepathy.

But first of all, astral travel can definitely be understood as a form of "telepathy with altered self-awareness".

However, there are quite increases to the basic telepathic and telekinetic experiments described so far, which can no longer be explained by the fact that there are analogous connections in the world besides the causal ones. In the phenomena described in the following the laws of nature are obviously suspended.

- A well-known case is the so-called "spontaneous healing", where a person suddenly cured an illness he had – often without knowing how exactly he did it. The cancer suddenly disappeared. Physically, this phenomenon cannot be explained at first – one can only diagnose it and give it the name "spontaneous healing".

- There is another variant of this phenomenon: healing by another person. The healer involved in this process also usually does not take any physical measures, but prays for healing, imagines the healing or performs other magical-religious measures.

- With a materialization suddenly an object appears, which was not there before. This does not mean a magic trick, but a real "appearance out of nothing". Of course, such a phenomenon is most convincing if you experience it when you are alone, when nobody else can have manipulated anything.

- The counterpart of materialization is de-materialization, i.e. "dissolving into nothingness". This phenomenon is described much less frequently than materialization. (I did not experience this myself up to now.)

- Another variant of the materialization is the matter-change. Here, as the name already says, the matter is changed. The most well-known example is certainly the transformation of water into wine by Jesus.

However, one can also consider spontaneous healing and healing by a healer as a matter change.

- Where best to classify the firewalk is a bit unclear. In a firewalk, one walks barefoot (without any aids!) over glowing coals – one can also lie naked in the embers for a while or eat some bits of embers. (I've done this myself.)

8

- A similar extreme form of telekinesis is e.g. the lifting of a truck by a mother, so that she can pull her child from under the wheel of the truck, under which the child got in an accident. In this case, the mother does not think that what she is doing is impossible.

Similar processes are known especially from karate and kung fu.

Also the long-distance pushes, i.e. the knocking over by telekinesis of a person who is some meters away, belongs to this sort of phenomena.

In addition to the type of healing described at the beginning, there is also the variant that the healer reaches into the body of the sick person with his hands and changes something there. Is this an extreme form of telekinesis? Or is this a matter-change? In the end, the matter-change belongs of course also to the telekinesis phenomena – it is only a rather extreme form of telekinesis.

Another variant of this extraordinary telekinesis are the healings of broken bones by the Australian Aborigines, who only concentrate and sing and play the didgeridoo for achieving this healing.

The phenomena described here can be classified into two categories, based on the assumptions necessary for their description:

Intensity-Forms of Magic	
causal-analogous world view	*laws of nature are suspended*
telepathy	simple telekinesis (paper wheel)
astrology	astral travel
oracle (tarot etc.)	materialization
foreseeing the future	de-materialization
random steering	matter transformation
bilocation	spontaneous healing
	healing by a healer
	firewalking

Essentially this distinction is a division into telepathy and telekinesis:

- For the description of telepathy an extended scientific world view is sufficient, in which there are also analogous connections, in which each event stands in a connection with all other events – as this is described among other things by astrology.

- For the description of telekinesis an extended scientific world view is not sufficient, because there are phenomena which contradict the laws of nature.

I 2.   Procedure

The second point is the procedure – can clear differences be found? And if so, what is the relation between the procedure and the magical phenomena caused by it?

There are two approaches to answering this question, but there is little difference between them: First, one's own experience as well as the experiences of people one knows very well; and second, the descriptions of the way saints, yogis, magicians, etc. have worked miracles. As a precaution, one should include these historical accounts in one's argument only if they agree with one's own experience.

First of all, there are a few forms of magic that are available to everyone without any preparation.

> - Just about everyone feels it when they are being stared at from behind. This form of telepathy was once necessary for survival in the Stone Age if you wanted to avoid being eaten by a hungry tiger sneaking up from behind. Therefore, the psyche has never suppressed this form of telepathy – just to make sure …

> - There is quite a large number of people who have dreamed at night what will happen the next day: temporal telepathy.

Then there are some forms of magic that anyone can perform and for which you need only a suitable experimental setup.

> - For using astrology, tarot, I Ching and other oracles, you just need to understand the oracle system and be able to combine a little.

> - For the realization of simple telepathy the postcard experiment is suitable. Just about any group of four people can experience telepathy this way. (I have yet to see a group that could not.)
> For this experiment, 10 different postcards are placed in 20 identical envelopes, which are then taped shut. Then a sealed envelope is placed on a table with four people sitting at it. These persons concentrate for about 3 minutes on the picture on the postcard (which they cannot see visually) and then note down all perceptions. Afterwards, the basic description of the picture is put together from the perceptions that at least three persons have had and then supplemented by the perceptions that two persons have had.
> If you can do this experiment with e.g. a whole school class, i.e. with several groups of four people each, the aha effect is still greater.

- The "paper wheel" experiment can also be done successfully by anyone. Initially, it may be necessary to perform it once with a person who has already mastered it.

The quite simple experimental arrangement can be found (as already said) in youtube e.g. on "psi-wheel".

So there are forms of magic for which no "previous training" or long practice is necessary.

However, with some forms of magic a "manual" is very helpful and shortens the learning very much:

- Dream journeys are a "very normal state of consciousness" – they are, so to speak, intentional daydreams. Anyone can learn them very quickly if they are done two or three times with someone who has practice. The practiced person is, so to speak, the training wheels on the dream journey bicycle for the unpracticed "student driver".

Again, you don't need a lot of practice, just instruction and some experience, because dream journeys are no longer firmly integrated into our culture.

For some forms of magic, a special inner attitude is necessary to make the spell in question effective:

- In talismanic magic and similar forms of magic, by which an object, a person, a circumstance, a situation, or the like is summoned, great concentration and imagination is necessary for the spell to work.

If you want to find a key that someone else has lost, or if you want to levitate a feather, this is usually not possible without long research and practice:

- Finding lost objects, recognizing (by dream travel) the shape of a plant of which one knows only the name, finding the solution to a criminal case, etc., that is, advanced telepathy, requires a greater degree of practice, by which one becomes more confident in terms of "inner vision" and is able to distinguish telepathic perception well from one's own associations, guesses, and imaginations.

As with all forms of telepathy, the essential trick is that you can recognize everything that comes "from outside" by the fact that it has no roots in your own psyche – you cannot trace a telepathic perception back into your own psyche. With an own thought, on the other hand, one can at least find the preliminary stage, i.e. the thought which preceded the own thought.

11

- The more extreme forms of telekinesis seem to have special preconditions in contrast to the more advanced forms of telekinesis – at least it is no longer sufficient to show someone how to do it or just to practice it for a while.

The only two people I have met who can do advanced telekinesis "on demand" are Daskalos and Frater U.D..

Daskalos healed the spine of a friend of mine, which was very crooked, with "laying on of hands" and straightened it so that she could become a full-time dancer afterwards. The radiographs of her spine before and after the healing looked very different. Unfortunately, I don't know how Daskalos did it – though I suspect that it is not a matter of a manual method, but of an inner attitude.

Frater U.D. has learned, among other things, long-distance thrusts, i.e. physically knocking over people standing a few meters away – without any physical contact. He said that you don't "do" it, but "let it happen" – again, there is no manual instruction.

I know of even more people who have mastered these remote thrusts, but I have not met them personally.

There is one striking feature in advanced telekinesis: one must let the magic work undisturbed, otherwise it cannot unfold. This characteristic can adopt various forms:

- Sometimes one wishes for something "in passing" without any emphasis, but also without any inner doubts about the wish and also without any inner contradiction to this wish. These wishes tend to come true very quickly. For me, this is always pretty much half an hour – no matter whether I wish for a second bicycle (for visitors for joint bicycle tours) or a relationship (I then got to know the woman after half an hour).

However, this only works if this wish is really completely relaxed and filled with a slight anticipation.

- In sigil magic, it is customary to concentrate first for a short time intensely on the symbol with which one sends out one's wish into the world, but then to forget about the symbol and the entire ritual after the end of the sending out.

This forgetting is a form of non-interference – one lets the wish work undisturbed. This corresponds to the relaxed anticipation and "not paying attention" in the previous method.

- A third method is found mainly in small spiritual communities such as yoga sects, witchcraft covens, magical orders, and the like. In these communities it is common to wish for everything you need – and to receive it. So the communities of Jesus-People sit down in the morning and write everything they need for that day on a piece of paper and ask Jesus in prayer to send them these things – which then happens.

Here, complete trust in a deity or the like takes on the task of ensuring that the wish can be realized without hindrance. Also complete trust does not cast doubt on the expressed wish – therefore it is not necessary to forget the wish.

These three methods show that at least a doubting mind can be a great disturbing factor in the practice of effective magic. The conviction that one's own magic will be successful, on the other hand, promotes the effectiveness of this magic. So what is needed for magic is also a clearity and single-mindedness that does not waver: a clearly directed intention that is coordinated and unambiguous like a laser beam.

Then there are some forms of magic that obviously contradict the laws of nature. Even with them, some regularities can be observed.

- In a firewalk one walks barefoot over 600-800° hot, glowing charcoals – at these temperatures every cutlet burns immediately … The interesting thing about firewalking is that there seem to be no rules – except that the right thing happens, i.e. what suits the firewalker in question.

I have tried to find out the rules of firewalking: You are supposed to pass over briskly – so I stopped in the middle of the embers; then I was told that this can only be done with the soles of my feet – so I took the embers in my hands and threw them up into the air; then I took off my clothes and lay naked in the embers (a brilliant experience!); then I played cherry pit spitting with pieces of embers; finally I ate pieces of embers … then I could think of no more new experiments …

I saw mostly people who voluntarily walked over the embers – but once a woman simply pulled her friend along, and in another case a three-year-old child simply followed her mother, although the child was supposed to keep standing in front of the embers. One woman did not take off her nylon stockings – no problem …

I have also seen that a woman who has been assisting firewalking for years fainted after walking over the fire – she had a blister on her foot that hurt so badly that she couldn't stand it anymore. After she regained consciousness, she fought the pain for another three hours until she finally burst into tears. As she said afterwards, this was the best thing that could have happened to her – she had never cried before because she had tried all her life to prove to her father that she was strong. This old psychic imprint dissolved by this fire-walking experience, so that the woman was clearly more alive afterwards.

There are also burnt feet – but so far I have seen this only once with a man who wanted to show off with his firewalk and show how big and great he is. It didn't work – which he was glad about afterwards.

One can consider the firewalk as a form of telekinesis, but it seems as if the reasons for its functioning or non-functioning would lie outside the intentions of the firewalker – the fire itself decides what it does, so to speak, and it seems to know what is good for the person concerned …

In any case, the functioning of a firewalk is in no way dependent on knowledge, practice, tricks and similar things.

- All the materializations I have experienced so far or have been told about by people whose sincerity and powers of observation I trust, have happened on purpose.

The chocolate bars that sometimes appear during spiritistic sessions appear without any special request for them. (I have heard about this many times.)

Sometimes during a ritual on the altar suddenly appear things that fit the ritual, but that were not there before.

I myself once placed a necklace with a golden Christ and a second necklace with a silver dragon on a public cobblestone square with the words "For the one for whom they are intended." I put them down because I felt that I had to let them go. After three months I went to that place again, but the chains were gone – gold and silver don't stay on the ground in a public place for three months … Then I looked around for a moment and when I looked again at that place on the ground, the two chains were there again … The one for whom they were intended was obviously myself. About this phenomenon of de-materialization and re-materialization one can say that it happened without intention, but it fitted to the situation. (The two necklaces cannot be "only" invisible for three month, for this place has been cleaned regularly.)

- If one looks in historical reports, one notices, among other things, that before each of his miracles, Christ thanked God that he would fulfill his wish. Obviously, Jesus was completely convinced that God would grant him his wish. A greater certainty, one-pointedness and unambiguity and a greater confidence are hardly imaginable. And his miracles have already turned the laws of nature quite thoroughly upside down: Healing the sick, walking on water, turning water into wine, bringing the dead back to life, etc. This thanks to God in advance is the only thing that can be recognized as a "method" – the magic itself then happened "just like that".

The same can be observed in the case of the prophet Elijah and his disciple Elisha: the parting of the floods of the Jordan, the transformation of poison into wine, the calling down of fire from heaven, the reviving of the dead, etc., also happened in these cases only by a simple gesture, which was usually connected with a request to God.

Also, if you look around India, you will see that the yogis, the mahasiddhis and other saints perform their miracles without any preparation, without ritual, without long texts, without concentration exercises, and the like. In some cases, these yogis, etc., simply showed their abilities to doubters in order to demonstrate to them the correctness of their own worldview.

The same is true of the magicians in the Germanic, Celtic, Finnish, Siberian, etc. traditions. The triggering of a great magical effect does not require a great external and internal action.

However, it is known about all these "miracle-performers" that they had previously gone through a period of meditation and retreat into solitude, after which they were able to perform miracles.

Three cases can be distinguished here:

1. Some materializations happen spontaneously.

2. In firewalking, one can consciously stretch the limits of what is possible more and more.

3. After a long period of practice, one can also perform miracles intentionally and purposefully.

There is one more element common to these miracles: all miracles were not performed for themselves, but for a higher purpose. Even my firewalking experiments were not for self-expression, but were on the one hand research and on the other hand simply tremendous fun.

I have found only two exceptions to this rule:

1. The prophet Elisha, after receiving a blessing from his teacher Elijah at his death, verified this blessing by commanding the river Jordan to stop and let it go dry through the riverbed to the other side – which the river did. This he has done to be sure that the blesswing had worked.

2. In battle magic, targeted long-distance blows without physical contact and the like are possible.

If there should be the rule that miracles always happen for the benefit of a greater whole, this would mean that self-defense (battle magic), research (Elisa, firewalking) and fun (firewalking) are also sufficient motivation. But maybe this point has to be formulated differently.

Six forms different forms of approach can be distinguished:

1. magic which is possible for everyone at any time:
   - warning telepathy (being stared at from behind)
   - future dreams (dreaming the events of the next day)

2. magic that is made possible by guidance:
   - telepathy ("picture in envelope" experiment).
   - telekinesis ("paper wheel" experiment)

3. magic that becomes possible by practice:
   - dream travel telepathy
   - talisman magic
   - sigil magic

4. magic that works without preparation but with great motivation:
   - spontaneous healings
   - healings
   - long-distance thrusts

5. magic that works by single-mindedness:
   - wishing something incidentally
   - forgetting the wish
   - trust the wish fulfillment completely

6. magic that is directed towards a superior goal (this point ist still unclear):
   - healing
   - enjoyment (turning water into wine)
   - research, knowledge
   - self-preservation
   - fun (firewalking)

It is noticeable that the telepathic phenomena are found at points 1, 2 and 3, while the telekinetic phenomena are found at points 2 to 6. Obviously, in magic, perception (telepathy) is easier to learn than action (telekinesis).

13. Experience

The third point, which can be examined after the phenomena and the procedure, is the subjective experience in the different kinds of magic.

- First of all, there are the two types of spontaneous magic, that is, the feeling of being stared at, and the truth dreams.

Being stared at leads to a diffuse restlessness and a searching looking around.

The dreams usually only lead to astonishment. Sometimes, when people wake up in the morning, they realizes that the dream was a future dream and that they will experience it today – but this is rather rare. Mostly, when they experience it during the day, they remember the dream from the previous night and realize only then that their dream has been a future dream.

- Also with the simple magic experiments like the one with the postcards in the envelopes or the one with the paper wheel there is usually astonishment at first, because the experience does not fit into the previous world view, but most people get used amazingly fast to the fact that these possibilities exist. Most people seem to be quite pragmatically inclined.

- Most people find practicing concentration and imagination rather annoying and therefore look for shortcuts. These simplifications include dream journeys (where one learns to imagine by the way), sigil magic (which requires only very brief concentration), and sexual magic (which facilitates concentration by coupling it with sexuality).

These exercises increase the effectiveness of the magic to a certain level, but then it cannot be increased any further.

- Using "wish-forgetting", trusting in a deity and "wishing just incidentally" increase the effectiveness of magic very significantly. At the same time, it becomes largely effortless.

- The subjective experience of "miracles" is not so easy to describe, because it is not easy to find and interview someone who can perform miracles …

From myself I know that there is a certain state of mind that precedes such events. It is a deep, non-contradictory sense of rightness. In this, I want something or desire something, but try not to force anything – it is more that I recognize that something would be right or is right. From this everything else

17

follows – from completely absurd coincidences (a big ocean wave washes a golden necklace to the front of my feet that looks exactly like the one I just wished for) to "laying naked in the fire" and materializations. I have also had this feeling of rightness during my firewalkings, which has sometimes increased to a feeling of great fun and mischievous joy. Sometimes it has also been the feeling of being part of something greater or of completely entrusting oneself to a deity.

One magician I have known for several decades has described the progression to the state of being able to perform extraordinary magic by experiencing being integrated into something greater – a deity or whatever you want to call that greater thing. He feels that in miracles he is not acting himself, but that something is acting through him.

In the accounts of yogis, mahasiddhis, medicine men, shamans, saints, founders of religions, etc., one always finds that they acted out of a deep conviction, out of a sense of rightness, and in complete trust in a teacher, guru, or deity when they performed their miracles. Naropa trusted in his guru Tilopa; Christ trusted in God, John the Baptist, Elijah and Moses; the Druids trusted in their teacher-Druid, etc.

Often there is also a line of transmission like "Buddha … Tilopa – Naropa – Marpa – Milarepa … Dalai Lama" or "Moses … Prophets … Elijah – Elisha … John the Baptist – Christ – Peter … Pope". Such lines of transmission consist of a first teacher and his disciple, who in turn has a disciple, who in turn has a disciple, and so on. In this process, the disciple is given "instruction and transmission of power". The teaching gives expertise and know-how, the transmission of power connects the student with a deity or the first teacher. The teaching is the apparatus, the power transmission is the power connection …

The distinctive element in the miracles, that is, in the extraordinary magic, is obviously the connection to something greater, which is preferably a deity.

I 4.   Tree of Life

To describe the entire Kabbalistic Tree of Life would become too extensive. The part of the Tree of Life that is important in this context is the so-called "Middle Pillar," which is the central part of the Tree of Life. It consists of five sections, one above the other:

Kether:	One God
Da'ath:	deity
Tiphareth:	soul
Yesod:	psyche
Malkuth:	body

Malkuth

In Malkuth, only the "normal" causal laws of nature operate – the body acts only in a causal way.

Yesod

In Yesod the simple magic works as well: recognizing to be stared at, truth dreams, telepathy and telekinesis with guidance and the like. Here also belongs the magic that can be obtained by practice. This is the realm of the psyche, t.e. the individual subconsciousness and of the life force.

Tiphareth

In Tiphareth is one's own soul – one experiences one's own center. In order to get there permanently, one must heal one's own psyche, i.e. free it from fears, addictions, contradictions, traumas and the like. The effect of this is well known to all magicians: With inner contradictions one cannot achieve unity and without this unity the effect of magic remains quite small – and the result of magic also contains the contradiction in motivation …

The inner freedom from contradiction, on the other hand, leads to clarity and one-pointedness and thus to a greater magical effect. In this state, one does exactly what one wants.

Da'ath

In Da'ath are the deities. Just as the psyche and the life force shape the body, so the soul shapes the psyche – and so a deity shapes the soul. The soul is, so to speak, a drop from the sea of a deity.

This relation of the soul (Tiphareth) to a deity (Da'ath) is shown in the extraordinary magic, that is seen in Da'ath magic in several places:

> - in the experience of finding one's own protective deity, i.e. the deity of which one's soul is a part,
> - in the transmission of power, i.e. in the establishment of the connection with a deity,
> - in the complete trust in a deity,
> - in becoming integrated into something greater,
> - in the feeling of rightness, i.e. of being in harmony with a deity, and
> - in the fact that in the miracles something acts through oneself.

Thus, it can be said that the basis of Da'ath magic is the connection to one's patron deity.

Since deities have a well-defined character but are demarcationless, the Da'ath realm is also boundless – therefore the effect of Da'ath magic is also boundless.

One can understand the basis of Da'ath magic as the permanent invocation of one's own protective deity or a general deity (Christ, Krishna, Allah, Shiva, Osiris, etc.). Devotion to this deity then leads to integration into this deity. While it is natural to integrate into one's own patron deity, self-integration into any deity brings one to the Da'ath state of detachment.

Da'ath is also the collective subconsciousness, that is the life force not mainly in oneself (as in Yesod) but in everything.

Kether

A form of Kether magic is not known to me – presumably in Kether one is simply what one is … and has no motivation whatsoever to change anything about it – changes are, after all, unthinkable in a state that is a unity, since there is no room for change there.

II The Character of Da'ath Magic

This so far still somewhat abstract description of Da'ath magic can be made more tangible with the help of some considerations and examples.

II 1. Foundation

First of all there are generally accessible or effective forms of the non-physical connections or effects:

- General forms of non-physical correlations are astrology, omens, and oracles, all of which show that there is an order of analogy in the world, i.e., that things are related to each other and evolve in unison.

This is not a compelling condition for the existence of a boundless state, but it fits well to such states. An analogical order in a boundless realm suggests that this realm has something organic about it – which would fit well with the idea of deities as the "items" of this boundless state.

- Special forms of the non-physical connections are simple telepathy (being stared at) and simple telekinesis (paper wheel).

They show that everybody has these abilities and that therefore probably all things will be connected also in this way. If we assume that all things, not only humans, are telepathically connected (also animals can feel the sensing and plants react to thoughts), then there is a kind of telepathic network of consciousness between all things.

The same should be true for telekinesis.

- In classical physics, especially in mechanics, all things are clearly separated and delimited from each other. This corresponds to viewing the world from a Malkuth point of view.

In modern physics, however, this delimitation no longer exists: Everything acts on everything, space and time are the two aspects of space-time (relativity), matter is "frozen energy" ($E=mc^2$), energy is a form of space-time, quanta are not firmly delimited, the Heisenberg uncertainty relation describes fuzzy transitions, below a certain size there is only the completely chaotic "quantum foam", in the elementary particle realm only statistical rules apply, but no more causality, etc.

This list could be continued and described in great detail – but the important thing is only that also in physics this Da'ath-level of boundlessness has been discovered.

II 2. Yesod and Da'ath

The best known term for the just described basis of the boundaryless state of consciousness is "collective subconsciousness". Telepathy and telekinesis are the perceptions and actions in the collective subconsciousness.

On the Kabbalistic Tree of Life, the realm of Yesod is the individual subconscious and Da'ath is the realm of the collective subconscious, i.e., the realm of the deities and the "superior beings." These "superior beings" are the group consciousness of, for example, all human beings, in which all present perceptions and all memories of previous perceptions are contained. This consciousness corresponds approximately to the Great Mother, the primeval man, the primeval giant or God.

To the Great Mother as the "group-consciousness" of the people correspond the animal mothers with the animals, which one can meet among other things on the dream journeys to the power animals. They are the white she-wolf, the white buffalo-woman, the white elephant etc.. These animal mothers are called "white" or sometimes "great", because in dream journeys they appear in the shape of the animal species in question, but on the one hand they around two times bigger and on the other hand they consist of a milky white, luminous mist. This white mist is the usual perception of the life force. It is sometimes called "smoke" and more rarely "light" or the like.

The deities of the humans and the animal mothers of the animals correspond to the elves in the case of the plants. They are the group consciousness of a plant species, the "superior being" of this plant species. They normally do not have the often depicted, cute or erotically touched shape of many elf depictions, but reflect the essence of the respective plant species.

In the case of minerals, these "superior beings" are found as dwarfs – although here, too, one should not imagine little men with beards and pointed hats.

The often human form of the "plant spirits" and the "stone spirits" are only translation of the essence of the group consciousness of this species, thus of their collective subconsciousness, into the human imagery. The animals as "moving beings" are obviously similar enough to the human beings not to have to be translated into a human form as a rule. Such transformations of animals into a human form occur only now and then: with the Egyptian animal deities, in dream journeys with power animals, in fairy tales, in myths etc. – but these are rather rare cases.

One also encounters these "superior beings" in the effect of homeopathic globules that one has taken – one connects with the collective subconsciousness of the animal species, plant species or stone species in question.

One can call the totality of these beings, i.e. the Great Mother of humans, the animal mothers, the plant elves and the mineral dwarfs, "Gaia", i.e. the entire, all-encompassing group consciousness of the Earth.

One can, of course, go beyond the earth and assume a cosmic collective subconsciousness, but normally one will not need to think that far.

II 3.   Boundlessness

Boundlessness is most clearly presented in Buddha's writings. According to Buddha, an enlightened person is characterized by four "boundless states":

- He has <u>boundless equanimity</u>, that is, he looks at all things and sees them as they are – without adding to them or taking away from them. He is sincere in his perception – he sees all things as they are. He is serene and accepts that the world is as it is – he does not delude himself. He no longer has any fears, addictions or traumas to cloud his view of the world. Therefore, his consciousness no longer contains only the images of his own psyche, but the images of the entire collective subconsciousness.

- He has <u>boundless compassion</u> because he has opened his perception to the entire world and also perceives the feelings of others. He has, so to speak, perfect telepathy – he is at home in the collective subconsciousness, he is fully awake in the collective subconscious, he is on a constant, all-encompassing dream journey.

- He has <u>boundless love</u> because he no longer perceives himself as separate from others. His frame of reference is no longer his own psyche (Yesod), but the collective subconsciousness (Da'ath). This gives rise to the motivation to help others as much as himself: his egoism, formerly limited to himself, has widened into a humanity-egoism. The striving for his own advantage has widened to a striving for the advantage of mankind, because he experiences himself as part of mankind – the collective subconsciousness has awakened in him and now acts through him for the advantage of mankind as a whole. The reason for this loving orientation is simply that he realizes that his own happiness will be greatest when all are happy – after all, he no longer experiences himself as an isolated psyche, but as the total psyche of humanity, that is, as the collective subconscious.

- He has <u>boundless joy</u>, because he experiences himself as part of the whole. Joy arises when something small vibrates together with something else and thereby a greater common vibration arises. This happens on the inside when one has reintegrated something that has been repressed, and it happens on the outside when one does something together with someone else. Now, when the psyche integrates into the collective subconscious, a particularly great joy arises because the collective subconscious is so large. Since so many new things are also constantly happening in it (the experiences of all people), this joy is also boundless because of what is constantly being added.

Similar descriptions can sometimes be found in the yoga scriptures or in the accounts of Christian mystics, Islamic Sufis, Kabbalists and the like.

A more comprehensive concept, encompassing not only human beings but all living beings, is found mainly in India in both Buddhism and Hindhuism. In Christianity such a view is rather an exception – the best known is still the sermon for the birds by St. Francis.

- A practical application of these possibilities of this expansion of consciousness is shown at the very end in the movie "Avatar", where a community ritual is shown, by which the consciousness of Jack Sully is transferred from his human body into his Avatar body.

This form of advanced magic is adapted from the "Phowa" from the "Six Yogas of Naropa" from Tibetan Buddhism. In the Phowa, the boundlessness is applied in a very concrete way, in that a dying Lama transfers his consciousness into the body of a young person who has just died, and then revives this new body and "inhabits" it for several more years.

II 4. Characteristics of the Da'ath State

Some characteristics of Da'ath magic, as well as of the state in which one can perform such magic, can be described after these considerations.

- First of all, people are one-pointed in Da'ath magic. However, this is a relaxed one-pointedness, that is, not the tense one-pointedness that comes from trauma or fanaticism. You know what you want, and you don't strain to achieve what you want – you just do it and it happens.

Practicing Da'ath magic is effortless – but the Da'ath state in which one can practice this kind of magic is not so easy to achieve.

- One experiences oneself as part of something greater, as something that has been integrated into something greater, as something through which something greater acts. One may call this "God" or "one's patron deity" or the "flow of life," but the idea here is always something greater out of which one exists and acts. Being in tune with this greater makes one's former magic become Da'ath magic.

A precursor to this is the feeling of being guided by God or by the deities – one begins to experience oneself as part of a continuum, as a firmly integrated part of the world.

- Every person has his own character, his own biography and his own horoscope and is therefore different from all others. This is not changed by the Da'ath state. However, two characteristics can be observed in people in the Da'ath state, which appear in the form that corresponds to the respective person: trust and responsibility.

This trust arises from the experience that one is part of the whole and is carried by the whole – the responsibility arises from the experience that one is part of the whole and therefore carries the whole.

These two qualities, however, as I said, can appear in quite different forms.

- Finally, there is something that could be called the "state of complete rightness": One does exactly what one wants without any restriction.

Some present this as a state they have found with difficulty by a healing, for others it is a martial state of self-assertion, for still others it is a gift from God … again, there are very many different interpretations of this state of rightness.

Sometimes it is also rewritten with the term "bliss".

Sometimes in the Da'ath state there is also an expanded awareness of one's own soul, in which the reincarnations of one's own soul become clearer. In this, one's "identity center" shifts from one's psyche to one's soul's intention for its current incarnation, then on to one's soul's awareness of all its incarnations, and finally to one's patron deity.

But this is a side effect of the Da'ath state rather than a central part of this consciousness or the magic that takes originates from the Da'ath state.

II 5. Types of magic

At this point, a brief overview may be helpful. The Middle Pillar of the Tree of Life describes five stages of development, which can also be found in magic – on the one hand in the way of perception and on the other hand in the possibilities of action. In addition, consciousness feels different at each of these five levels.

1st level: Malkuth
    a) realm: multiplicity
    b) part of being: body
    c) consciousness: waking consciousness
    d) perception:
        - One perceives with the sense organs, especially with the eyes (light rays are perceived by the eye).
        - The external world is perceived.
    e) action: One acts with the physical body in the physical world.

2nd stage: Yesod
    a) realm: the organic
    b) part of being: psyche
    c) consciousness: subconsciousness
    d) perception:
        - One perceives as in a dream: a diffuse light illuminates everything, the images are gray with little color, everything moves.
        - One perceives the inner world (and thus indirectly the outer world). This happens with the help of telepathy (perception of the life force).
    e) Action: One acts with the help of the life force, i.e. with the help of telekinesis in the area of the life force. In this case, one acts either without practice or one has practiced directing the life force and acts much more effectively with the help of concentration and imagination, using rituals, sigils, etc. as aids. By magic, one achieves individual, small goals that do not necessarily have to be in harmony with other goals of one's own.

3rd level: Tiphareth
  a) realm: the center
  b) part of being: the soul
  c) consciousness: deep sleep
  d) perception:

> - One sees colored still images, which are luminous from within and which rarely move. (The preliminary stage to this in the transition from the psyche to the soul contains images that are luminous, colorful, constantly transforming and flowing, and also have extremely sharp contours).
>
> - One perceives the essence of things, e.g. one's own soul.

  e) action: One acts out of one's soul, one acts in harmony with one's soul. By this one is one-pointed – after the encounter with one's own soul it becomes easier to dissolve inner contradictions, traumas, etc., so that one stands no longer in one's own way. By this unambiguity and single-mindedness, one's own magic becomes clearly more effective – one no longer wants to go left and right at the same time. In addition, the conscious anchoring of one's own psyche in one's soul and the support of the psyche in one's own soul gives magic a great additional boost – "One goes one's way calmly and unperturbed." In the process, the "coincidences" fit in such a way that one is able to go one's way. All magical actions are organic parts of one's being and are in harmony with each other.

4th level: Da'ath
  a) realm: continuum
  b) part of being: protective deity
  c) consciousness: collective subconsciousness
  d) perception:

> - One sees luminous, colorful figures in the light – they can generally be called "deities" or, if one prefers, "archetypes."
>
> - That which one perceives is the collective subconsciousness, that is, the continuum consciousness.

  e) action: One acts in accordance with rightness, something acts through oneself, one acts in perfect trust in something greater – usually this is one's own patron deity. By this "being embedded in something greater" also one's own "ordinary magic" (Yesod) becomes "extraordinary magic" (Da'ath), by which the laws of nature can be temporarily suspended to a much greater extent: Firewalkings, materializations, levitations, substance transformations, etc.

5th level: Kether

a) realm: unity

b) part of being: God

c) consciousness: all-encompassing consciousness

d) perception:

- One sees either an undivided glistening white light or a shining blackness – but both have the same properties. (The precursor to this is something that might be called a "light storm".)

- One sees the underlying unity of multiplicity.

e) action: One acts as the whole – however that may feel concretely …

III The Necessity of Da'ath Consciousness

The principle of continuum does not only exist in magic, but also in many other fields – the principle of continuum (i.e. Da'ath) is just about the most formative topic in the present time. Thus the considerations to the Da'ath magic and above all a possible collective reaching of a Da'ath state (including Da'ath magic) have a large and current importance.

- Since approx. 1900 A.D. a new world view has gradually emerged, in which space and time are no longer separated from each other (relativity theory), in which all elementary particles are at the same time also a wave (quantum physics), in which the physical properties of a particle are no longer exactly defined (Heisenberg's uncertainty relation), in which below a certain particle size there are only probabilities, but no more causality (quantum foam), etc.

In this world view, space-time is the only real thing – everything else including particles and energy are forms ("curvatures") of this space-time. Thus the world is seen from today's physical world view finally a continuum.

- Since about 1900 A.D. the psyche of the human being has been investigated, by which on the one hand it became clear how much the destinies of the individual human beings are intertwined with those of the other human beings, and on the other hand that all human beings have a common subconsciousness (collective subconsciousness).

The basis of people's psyches is also a continuum: the collective subconsciousness.

- In politics, the emergence of a collective mind, that is, the draft of a continuum worldview, came about as a result of the two world wars – that is, at about the same time as modern physics and psychology. Usually this worldview is called "global thinking".

This world view began with the foundation of the UNO and the EEC (today: EC) and has received quite fast several new facets by the danger of self-destruction of humans by the atomic bombs, by the extinction of species, by environmental pollution, by global warming, by overpopulation etc..

- The same principle is also found in the national economy. The former free market economy had created such an inequality that since about 1870 attempts were made to create a people-friendly form of economy with the

31

help of the social market economy and with the help of the planned economy (communism).

However, the previous approaches are not yet sufficient for this, since the general money fixation and the all-important competition principle still prevent a meaningful action and an effective cooperation. An economic system is needed that is based on cooperation and not on competition.

(A more detailed description may be found in my book "From Inner Abundance to Outer Prosperity").

- In relationships, too, there are beginnings of a continuum model. The lifelong monogamy is still the predominant model, but at the latest since the hippie era around 1968 there are many more flexible relationship models that are being tested. Out of the need to find forms suitable for everyday life, the model of the patchwork family, among others, has developed.

The three basic principles of these new forms of relationships are 1. sincere self-expression, 2. the free, flexible organization of relationships, and 3. co-operation, which also makes several relationships possible at the same time.

(A more detailed description may be found in my book "Love and Independence").

By comparing the basic structures in physics and in magic, it becomes apparent that both world views are parts of a larger whole:

> 1. The character of the angles in physics corresponds exactly to the character of the angles ("aspects") in astrology.

> 2. The structure of a superstring (that is the structure of an elementary particle or energy quantum) corresponds exactly to the structure of the zodiac.

> 3. The mathematical model, with which the superstring theory, i.e. the whole modern physics is described, corresponds exactly to the kabbalistic tree of life.

It can hardly be shown more clearly that physics and magic describe two sides of the same world. However, the description of a comprehensive physical-magical world view is still in its infancy. However, it is foreseeable that also this world view will be a continuum – after all, the world is a continuum from the point of view of physics as well as from the point of view of magic.

(A more detailed account may be found in my book "The Synthesis of Physics and Magic").

- In magic, the first models of a Da'ath magic are currently emerging. This Da'ath magic can be seen as a part of the general Da'ath consciousness, thus as an element of the new "epoch of globalization" beginning since about 1900.

One aspect of this Da'ath magic that has not yet been explicitly mentioned is that it is a permanent magic and not a punctiform magic as before. In a continuum, magic is constantly operative and it is also constantly conscious – it is a normal everyday element.

If you look at the development of civilization and worldview, the development of a continuum worldview is a logical and necessary step.

In the Paleolithic, people lived as part of nature in nature. This corresponds to the symbiosis of the baby with its mother. This is the simple "Yes" of the oral phase.

In the Neolithic period, one lived on the islands of culture (village, agriculture, animal husbandry) in nature. This corresponds to the infant's learning of demarcation when learning to walk and talk. This is the decisive "No!" of the anal phase.

In the era of kingship, everything was centrally controlled. This corresponds to the child experiencing itself as an acting person. This is the vehement "I!!!" which results from the synthesis of the "Yes" of the oral phase with the "No!" of the phallic phase.

In materialism everything is explored and used. This corresponds to the adolescent who explores himself, the world and sexuality. This is the searching "You?" of the genital phase.

In the era of globalization, sustainable structures are developed. This corresponds to the founding of a family. This is the reliable "We." which results from the synthesis of the "I!!!" with the "You?" in the adult phase.

In the future, another phase follows, which corresponds to the older person, whose children have left home, who discovers new things and becomes a teacher. This is the enriching "Other …" of the tutorial phase.

Finally, another phase follows in the far future, corresponding to the old person. This is the wise "All" that results from the synthesis of the "We." with the "Other …" in the gerontal phase.

(For a more detailed account, see my book "Die sieben Schritte des Lebens").

It is to be hoped that mankind will grow up collectively as soon as possible and behave like a family, so that mankind does not extinguish itself or make the earth uninhabitable. For this to happen, most people would have to be anchored in themselves and make the attitude of the "Earth family" their basic attitude – that is, achieve Da'ath consciousness, at least in its basic features.

IV   Practical Instructions for Da'ath Magic

This is the most important part of this book – the mere knowledge of a theory, which has not been successfully put into practice, does not change one's life very much.

Unfortunately, there is no magic formula for achieving the Da'ath state and Da'ath magic. Everyone has to find his own way and his own style. However, one can describe the landscape through which all these paths lead – even if, of course, everyone sees this landscape through the glasses of his own horoscope again a little differently … In this landscape there are all kinds of attitudes and actions that are conducive to the achievement of the Da'ath state. And there are also basic experiences that probably everyone will encounter …

The following chapters are arranged in such a way that they build on each other – but this refers only to their presentation and not to a logical and necessary order of experiences, since everyone goes through this landscape to Da'ath in his or her very own way.

IV 1.   Resolution

A journey begins in most cases with a decision – however, one can also suddenly reach the Da'ath state unplanned by a meditation, a ritual, an encounter or any other experience. The usual case, however, is the deliberate setting out on the journey – even though one may not see quite clearly where the resolved journey will lead and what one will experience on it.

IV 1. a)   Invitation of the Da'ath state

If one finds it very tempting to learn about the extraordinary magic that is firmly connected to one's own soul and to the gods, then it is helpful to make a resolution and to depict and anchor it in a ritual.

This ritual can be quite simple: One stands, addresses one's words to one's own soul, to the gods, to life, and states as clearly as possible what one wants to achieve. As always with such proclamations of will, it is helpful to have a witness present – this gives the process much more grounding.

One can expand this ritual in various ways – by a suitable place, a suitable time, by

35

special (ritual) clothing, etc., but one can also make this resolution spontaneously on a lonely walk in the woods.

What is important about this resolution is its grounding – its effect is as great as its roots are deep.

At first, only the decision is important, one does not need to know one's own path at this time – the path will only become visible in the course of the walk …

Such a decision usually has a more or less conscious prehistory:

>There has first been something that caused one pain, or there has been something that seemed very tempting.

>Then one has looked at the pain or the temptation and accepted its existence and no longer pushed it aside. Thus it has consciously become one's own pain or desire.

>Third, one has then found hope that the goal might be attainable – to end the pain or to achieve the attrative state or thing. Nobody goes a way which he considers impossible …

>The fourth step is the decision to go, which can be expressed and grounded ritually in front of one or more witnesses.

>Then follows as fifth the actual way, which has two aspects:

>>- inwardly a meditation or similar, which keeps the resolution clear and awake and alive, and

>>- outwardly the going of the next useful step. When one has taken this step, one looks where one is and takes another useful step …

In this way begins the inner development and the outer wandering, which finally leads to the goal.

IV 2.   Getting to know

If one wants to achieve something, it is useful to get to know this goal more closely and to become familiar with this state. There are several ways to do this (as is usually the case).

IV 2. a)   Witnessing miracles

In order to experience how extraordinary magic and thus the Da'ath state feels, the easiest thing to do is to watch a miracle once.

The only such event that is relatively easy to specifically seek out is a firewalk. Other such "hair-raising" events like materializations or surgeries with bare hands, where the operated person feels no pain and the surgical wound heals immediately afterwards, cannot be booked as easily as a firewalk as a seminar.

Therefore, participation in a firewalk is a good start. A big advantage of the firewalk is that you are right in the middle of this hot business and experience it first hand …

Maybe you can also find someone who is so far advanced in battle magic that he can perform e.g. long distance thrusts. However, the participation in a firewalk is the easiest to carry out, because for this a short look in the internet is enough.

However, there is a second way to witness miracles, which is also quite easy to implement.

Imagine Christ going to a mountain after the feeding of the 5000 to meditate and pray. While doing so, one walks next to Christ and feels into him in order to experience in which inner condition he is. Afterwards, Christ goes to the Sea of Galilee and walks across the water to the boat of his disciples. You walk next to Christ in your imagination and feel into him again. If you wish, you may ask Christ if it is all right with him if you change into him with your consciousness in order to be able to experience more directly what he is doing while waking on water. In this way, you can get a first taste of what it is like when someone performs a miracle.

The same can be done with all the other cases where someone has performed extraordinary magic. The following list contains only a few examples of such miracles out of several traditions:

- Naropa walks on water
- Christ raises Lazarus to life
- Elijah calls down fire from heaven

- Elisha separates the floods of the Jordan
- Moses calls forth a spring
- Sai Baba materializes various things
- Apollonius of Tyana raised a dead woman to life
- Medea dismembered and revived a ram
- an Egyptian magician transformed a wax crocodile into a real crocodile
- an Egyptian magician revived a decapitated man
- Milarepa levitates
- Rumi walks through the air

This list could be continued for a long time. Of course, one can ask whether all these stories are true, whether they are to be understood only allegorically, whether they are merely myths, etc. However, the essential point in connection with learning Da'ath magic is not primarily the question of the historical authenticity of the various reports, but above all whether one can learn something about miracles from the "inner witnessing" of these events – and this can only be found out by witnessing them in a dream journey.

The academic discussion about the genuineness of these events does not help very much – the co-experiencing however could lead to the one or other realization. If one should find out, for example, that all these men and women who have performed miracles have been inwardly in the same state of consciousness, then it would be worthwhile to strive for this state oneself.

This state of consciousness is completely one-pointed, full of trust and distinction – and also completely serene, relaxed and independent.

Of course, one can also ask oneself whether it might make sense to watch wizards at work who are merely characters in novels such as Gandalf, Saruman, Dumbledore, Master Yoda and so on. Well – try it out …

IV 2. b) Dream journeys

The Sephirah ("sphere") Da'ath on the Kabbalistic Tree of Life represents the realm from which the extraordinary magic originates. It is therefore obvious to make a dream journey to Da'ath once and to see what one experiences there, how the world looks from this point of view.

Of course, one can also undertake dream journeys to other symbols of this realm or state, such as the Gate of Heaven, the Beyond River and the Beyond Bridge.

This method sounds very simple, but it can be extremely effective. It may be even more effective if two or three people undertake a dream journey to Da'ath.

IV 2. c) Invocation

Invocation is a method by which one can obtain an intense contact with a deity. Since the living beings or, if one wants to express it more technically, the "consciousness units" in a continuum (Da'ath) are deities, the contact with a deity is also a way to get to know the Da'ath state.

For such an invocation, one should choose a deity to which one is already attracted – this makes the contact easier.

First of all, you can look at pictures of this deity and study its myths. Either afterwards or even before that, one can then undertake dream journeys to this deity – this will make the deity much more alive in one's own consciousness.

The simplest invocation can be done inside a dream journey by asking the deity if one may cross over into its consciousness. By doing so, one can then see the world from that deity's point of view and experience oneself as that deity.

In the classical invocation, one begins by describing the deity and imagining it as standing in front of oneself. In doing so, one also imagines what one is describing: "She is ..." Then one moves on to addressing the deity directly and recounting its deeds, for example: "You are ..." Finally, one shifts over to the imagined image of the deity and speaks as that deity, voicing what one wants to accomplish oneself: "I am ..." or "I do ..."

In the more archaic forms of invocation, the invoker dresses like the deity and puts on an appropriate mask: The mask of the great predator in hunting spells, the mask of the jackal god Anubis in the mummification ritual, the ancestor masks in the dances of the North American Indians, the mask of the monkey god Hanuman in the Onam celebration, etc.

When in a group ritual a single person masquerades and disguises as a deity, the "pressure" on the person to really change with his consciousness into this deity is quite great.

Some invocations can also be performed in special ways: The Egyptian shaman-god Bes may be invoked by dancing while beating the frame drum like him; the Greek god Pan may be invoked by dancing while playing a pan flute like him; the Celtic god-father Dagda or the Germanic poet-god Bragi may be invoked by playing the harp like them; Shiva may be invoked by a free ecstatic dance or by a fixed ritual dance; Osiris may be invoked by lying down in a coffin like him; etc.

If there is such a special and distinctive invocation method for a deity, it will usually be the most effective one.

As is generally the case, people have looked for "shortcuts" and "technical solutions" and experimented with drugs. In a traditional setting and under the guidance of experienced shamans or priests, this method seems to be quite effective, but for people who are outside such a tradition and just want to use the corresponding drug on their own, this method is at least very tricky, if not dangerous.

In any case, the question arises why one would want to achieve something with the help of drugs that one can just as well achieve without them – and without the unpleasant side effects that most drugs have …

IV 2. d)   Patron deity

One's own patron deity may be encountered on dream journeys, on vision quests, by the help of another person who already knows his or her patron deity, and so on. This deity is also called by other names. The underlying idea is that one's soul is a "drop" from the "sea" of a deity. This deity is, so to speak, the part of the continuum (Da'ath) out of which one's soul has encapsulated itself into a delimited being.

Knowing this deity is important in that it is the natural and most organical way into the continuum of Da'ath.

Possibly one has always felt attracted to this deity, perhaps it is closely related to one's own power animal (ibis – Thot; crocodile – Sobek; buffalo – Pte-san-win; monkey – Hanuman etc.), possibly it shows itself to oneself spontaneously in a special situation. Probably the easiest way to get to know one's own patron deity is to make a dream journey with the aim "to my patron deity".

Probably it makes sense to take your time until you come to the conclusion that a certain deity is your own patron deity. If it is, it will gradually become apparent as one discovers more and more similarities between one's own character and the nature of this deity.

It is not necessary to be able to explain conclusively why a particular deity must be one's own patron deity; the important point is the guidance and help and inspiration that a deity gives oneself – no matter what one's relationship to it may be.

For all practical purposes, it can be said that finding a deity you feel a kinship with and trust is very helpful on the path to Da'ath.

If it is the patron deity, invocations of that deity will be easily for oneself, they will feel natural, and one will feel that one is coming home.

IV 3.   Opening

If one wants to pass from the delimited realm of "ordinary magic" to the boundless realm of "extraordinary magic," it is obviously necessary to open one's boundaries …

This is a central element for the attainment of Da'ath magic. By the methods described in the previous chapter, one may have at least already experienced the taste of this state – and will very likely have gained an appetite for more as a result.

IV 3. a)   Extension of elemental magic

In occidental magic, the four elements plus the quintessence (light) are the usual division in magic – they appear in the pentagram ritual, in talismanic consecrations, in the Tarot cards, and so on. They even still characterize a large part of today's fantasy novels, where they appear, for example, as the four "houses" in the "Harry Potter" books.

One way of opening or widening the "ordinary magic" is therefore to look at the extraordinary forms of the element magic with the help of dream journeys. For this purpose, one again travels inwardly with the help of a dream journey to one of the events listed below and looks at it up close and feels again into the one who performs this magic.

Also here one usually does not know whether it concerns reports about real events or myths. Therefore, here too, only the dream journey itself shows whether one can learn something by "experiencing" these (real or mythical) events.

1st Earth:

- A Germanic sorceress triggers a landslide in the Gisli saga.
- Two different Germanic sorcerers trigger a landslide in the Styrbjörnar saga and the Landnama book, respectively.
- In the saga about Thorstein Viking's son, a wizard dives into the earth as into water. The same is reported in the Rafnista sagas about a wizard.
- Jesus multiplied bread and fish.
- Jesus healed the sick.
- Alchemists turned lead into gold.

2nd water:

- Jesus walked on water.
- Naropa walked on water.
- Moses parted the floods of the Red Sea.
- Moses made a spring in the desert.
- Baldur made a spring in Denmark.
- Elijah separated the floods of the Jordan.
- Elisha separated the floods of the Jordan.
- Jesus changed water into wine.

3rd air:

- The Druid-Bard Taliesin has caused a storm by a spell.
- Germanic lore is full of wind spells (Gesta danorum, Sverri saga, Ragnarsdrapa, Skaldskaparmal, Sörli saga and many others). This is because the Vikings, as sailors, depended on good wind.
- The Tibetan yogi Milarepa flew through the air.
- The Sufi Rumi floated through the air.
- Many Christian saints levitated ("hovered") while praying.

4th fire:

- Elijah calls down fire from heaven.
- Generally, firewalks are forms of fire magic.

5th light:

- Jesus revived Lazarus.
- Medea revived a slaughtered ram.
- Egyptian magicians revived animals.

These examples are again only a small selection of the miracles that can be found in the various traditions.

IV 3. b) The transition from Chesed to Da'ath

The attainment of Da'ath is a very striking experience. On the Kabbalistic Tree of Life, one usually passes from the realm of "Chesed" to the realm of Da'ath. In Chesed, although all things are still separate from each other, all things are visible – the boundaries become information-permeable, so to speak. Or in other words, everything becomes transparent. Chesed is also the realm where one can find one's soul's memory of its previous incarnations. This area is sometimes also called the "Akashic Chronicle."

If one goes one step further from Chesed, the boundaries dissolve completely. The boundaries are then not only transparent, but disappear completely. This is often experienced as a leap into a bottomless abyss – that is why the transition to Da'ath is also called "abyss". When all boundaries dissolve, one floats, so to speak, in nothingness ... the forest path under one's feet suddenly turns into the darkness between the stars ...

Therefore, if one wants to reach Da'ath, one has to let go of everything: the ground on which one stands, any external support, the boundary of one's own being ... In Da'ath, one can no longer define one's own individuality by a boundary between "I" and "non-I" – threre one can define one's own individuality only by one's own quality. Accordingly, also deities have no boundary, but only a clear quality – therefore also 500 people can call Pan, invoke Shiva or ask Christ for help at the same time ... this is no problem for the boundaryless consciousness of a deity.

In physics Da'ath is the realm of energy quanta – Chesed is the realm of elementary particles. Below the abyss there is matter, above the abyss only energy. So, crossing the abyss towards Da'ath corresponds to the transformation of matter into energy. The enormous intensity of this transformation process can be illustrated by the glow of the sun or by an atomic bomb. Correspondingly intensive is also the magic when one reaches Da'ath ... just extraordinary magic, Da'ath magic, miracles ...

IV 3. c) A Da'ath ritual

When one arrives unprepared at the "abyss" where all demarcations dissolve, one can suffer a more or less great shock ... it is as if one abruptly loses all hold and, moreover, sees all things that exist – normally no psyche can accept this calmly. Fortunately, it is not so easy to get to this inner place, where this happens – and if you perform the appropriate meditations, you can definitely reach the abyss without suffering a huge shock.

The prerequisite for this is a one-pointed consciousness that lasts for a long time. Probably the easiest way to describe this is by means of an example – and the obvious example for me is of course my own experiences with the abyss ...

When I was accepted by Axel as a sorcerer's apprentice about 43 years ago (I've been 22 at that time), I was still in civilian service and cycled a good hour every morning and every evening to the old people's home where I was on nursing duty. Since the winter was quite cold at that time, I froze badly on

43

my bike – especially my hands got icy every time despite wearing gloves. Then I had the idea to do something with the help of magic against the cold.

So I imagined that with every breath I breathe fire into my hands. When I breathed in, I imagined that I was drawing fire from the earth's interior or from the engines of passing cars, and when I breathed out, I let this fire glow in my hands. I then coordinated my breathing with my pedaling. Both while inhaling and exhaling, I inwardly spoke the word "fire".

With this meditation I was able to keep my hands warm enough that it was no longer uncomfortable.

So I had a rhythm of movement, a matching rhythm of breathing, a matching mantra also connected with it, then the constant imagination of fire coupled with it and finally as an important ingredient a very high concentration – because I wanted to avoid the pain of the icy cold in my hands.

After a few days I noticed that I had entered another state of consciousness. I didn't have a word for it at that time and had never heard that such a thing even existed. It was another state of consciousness in the sequence "deep sleep – dream – awakening – state X". It was a complete fulfilment, a smile, an inner warmth, a causeless happiness ... simply brilliant! Today I would call this state "one-pointedness" or "ecstasy".

This state can also be found in the EEG: Deep sleep has an EEG frequency of 3Hz, the dream state has 6Hz, waking has 12Hz and ecstasy has 24Hz. So I had also correctly grasped the order of these four basic states of consciousness.

After a few weeks I needed only one minute on the bicycle to get into this state – at that time riding a bicycle was my favorite activity ...

After a few months, I heard the inner call "Jump!" on my bicycle just before a busy intersection and inwardly saw a bottomless abyss in front of me. I panicked and sped away on my bike as fast as I could ...

A few hours later it dawned on me that I had obviously encountered a second new state of consciousness, of which I also had never heard anything before.

Much later it occurred to me that I had made quite exactly the Tibetan Tummo-meditation: breath-rhythm, fire-imagination, a very high concentration – and the whole thing is a protection against the cold ...

Obviously, the Tummo meditation is also meant to reach this state of one-pointedness and from there on to go on to the detachment of Da'ath. In the Tibetan yoga systems, such as in the "six yogas of Naropa", the awakening of the Kundalini fire, i.e. the Tummo meditation, is therefore the basis of all other meditations.

Thus, the question arises, in a very practical way, what one can do to dissolve the fear of dissolving any delimitation, before one day standing on the edge of this abyss, beyond which lies the realm of Da'ath. After years of futile questioning of healers, lamas, monks, roshis and the like, I finally found a way myself, which by its structure (as I later realized) is a Tibetan mandala meditation. It seems that the Tibetan Buddhists know this demarcationless area (and also the magic there) best.

This mandala meditation is a kind of transformation ritual. It is structured as follows:

> You can start with the Small Pentagram Ritual, in which Air is assigned to the east, Fire to the south, Water to the west, and Earth to the north. In the center is the light. These "4+1" elements and the pentagram ritual based on them are one of the most important foundations of occidental magic and therefore a good foundation for a mandala.

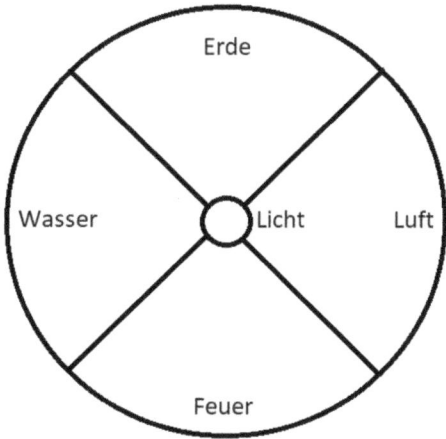

Now follows a more detailed consideration of the four elements, which one transfers into the most different areas of life, in order to be able to find them if possible in all things again:

Air	- East	- Morning	- Spring	- Thought	- Truth …
Fire	- South	- Noon	- Summer	- Will	- Power …
Water	- West	- Evening	- Autumn	- Feeling	- Love …
Earth	- North	- Night	- Winter	- Body	- Thriving …

Now consider these elements also in themselves:

Air:	breath, oxygen, flatulence …
Fire:	body heat, oxidation processes, sweating …
Water:	blood, saliva, urine …
Earth:	bones, fingernails, hair …

It is very helpful to undertake dream journeys to the four elements, since thereby living pictures of the four elements develop in oneself.

Next, consider the 12 possible transformations of the four elements as found in nature:

Water becomes Air:	fog, steam, clouds
Earth becomes Fire:	combustion
Earth becomes Water:	melting
Air becomes Water:	dew
Fire becomes Earth:	ash
Water becomes Earth:	freezing
etc.	

After that, you look at the 12 possible transformations of the four elements as you can find them in your own psyche:

Water becomes Fire:	love gives strength
Air becomes Earth:	expertise makes successful
Fire becomes Air:	strength gives the courage to see the truth
Earth becomes Fire:	Thriving strengthens the body
Water becomes Air:	love makes sincere
Fire becomes Earth:	strength creates facts
etc.	

Next, one considers all these transformations in their totality as a great flow of emerging and passing forms. By this one finally comes to the perception that there is only one underlying something that appears in constantly new forms – this is the light in the center of the mandala, the quintessence, the substance of the continuum, Da'ath …

This simple meditation can help one to move from the fixed division into the four elements, by multiple transformations, finally to the boundlessness between the four elements and thus to the quintessence.

If one finds it helpful, one can also stand or sit in the center of the element mandala of the pentagram ritual for this meditation. This concrete spatial assignment facilitates the concentration, makes the idea of the transformations as paths from one direction to another more vivid and places oneself from the beginning onwards in the center, i.e. in the place of the quintessence, which one ultimately wants to reach.

The effectiveness of this mandala meditation or mandala ritual depends on the intensity with which one performs it – that is, on the one hand, on how thoroughly one places the entire world and the contents of one's own psyche into the mandala of the four elements, and on the other hand, on how thoroughly one imagines the transformations of the four elements into the respective three other elements.

IV 3. d)   The way to the center

One can also use the Tree of Life or just the Middle Pillar as the basis for a meditation or ritual, marking it on the ground and then walking step by step from Malkuth to Da'ath.

One can also represent these five stages or steps as a mandala:

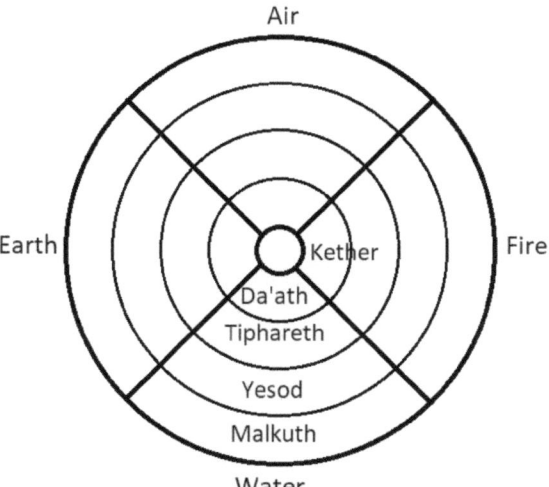

Whether one uses the previous, simple "Four Elements" mandala or this somewhat more complex mandala depends on how much detail or how much simplicity one feels most comfortable with in a meditation or ritual.

This mandala may be used in the same way as the previous mandala as a "transformational structure" and also as a path inward to Da'ath (and onward to Kether).

(A detailed description of mandalas and their use may be found in my book "Mandalas for Beginners").

IV 4. Development

One can certainly get to Da'ath in one leap (as I have experienced during my fire meditation on my bicycle), but a gradual approach is generally preferable, as it saves one from shock experiences that can make it difficult to return to that state.

IV 4. a) Kundalini

One of the most effective methods of reaching the Da'ath state, and thus Da'ath magic, is the awakening of one's Kundalini. Now this is not a topic that could be described in detail on three pages. Therefore, here is only a brief description of the Kundalini and a guide for beginners.

Kundalini is a part of the life force flowing in one's own body. This flowing life force can be seen as an equivalent to the blood circulation in the physical body. The life force rises inside the body like the jet of a fountain, unfolds above the head like the fountain of a waterspout fountain, then falls down around the body like the drops of a fountain, and then gathers again in the root chakra like the lake in which the fountain is located.

The kundalini is the rising ray of the life force. The fountain is sometimes depicted as seven serpent heads above the top of the meditator's head – the seven heads symbolizing the seven main chakras. The drops correspond to the outer rim of the aura.

To awaken the kundalini, one can begin with a simple meditation: inhaling, one imagines inhaling life force and directing it to the root chakra – inwardly speaking "fire". When exhaling, imagine that the life force is glowing in the root chakra – again saying "fire" inwardly.

If by this meditation no more new phenomena occur, one can additionally imagine a red, glowing cone, with its tip pointing upwards, in one's root chakra.

When you stimulate the Kundalini to rise more and with greater intensity, it pushes against all the blockages that you still have inside: memories, pains, cramps, fears, blocked anger, traumas, and so on. By the pressure that the rising Kundalini exerts against these blockages, these blockages become conscious.

At this point there is the possibility to simply increase the pressure more and more and to simply endure the arising feelings – then the thing happens, that is called the "black night of the mystics", the "raven head phase", the "afterlife journey" etc.

However, it seems to me to be more sensible to turn to everything that arises during this meditation. There are three steps: "look, feel, embrace". By looking closely at what appears in one's inside, one gets to know it. By feeling it, one connects with that part of one's own psyche and allow the old feelings trapped in it to become free again and to move. By finally embracing these parts of one's psyche, one reintegrates them.

By this process, one gradually dissolves all the things that one would otherwise see and experience all at once, unprepared, in Da'ath, where there are no more boundaries and thus nothing hidden.

By the gradual approach one avoids the shock at the first encounter with Da'ath.

Of course, one can already get to know Da'ath by dream journeys and on these dream journeys enjoy this Da'ath state without boundaries, but the probability that sooner rather than later one will also get to know in Da'ath all the shadows that are still hidden in oneself is nevertheless very high.

(A detailed description of the Kundalini and its dynamic and awakening may be found in my book "Kundalini for Beginners").

IV 5. Attitude

The continuum consciousness of Da'ath needs a certain attitude as a foundation or has a certain attitude as a consequence. By striving for this attitude, one gradually approaches the Da'ath state and thus Da'ath magic.

IV 5. a) One-pointedness

Even ordinary magic works best when one is one-pointed – in extraordinary magic I know of no case that has not had a complete one-pointedness as its basis.

This one-pointedness can look different, but it is always to be found: trust in God, trust in rightness, a completely relaxed desire, a definite will, an all-important will to survive, a calm matter-of-factness in doing something impossible, the complete lack of inner contradictions, and so on.

To achieve this one-pointedness, a complete self-affirmation is obviously necessary, or at least a complete unambiguity in what one is about to do. Consequently, one-pointedness originates from becoming familiar with one's motivations and resolving any contradictions in them.

The North Indian Buddhist yogis of a thousand years ago, called "Mahasiddhis," seem to have explored the attainment of one-pointedness most thoroughly. They developed various methods for this purpose.

One of them was called "removing water in the ear with water". The basis of this method is the same as in Yudo: one uses the power of the opponent to achieve one's own goal.

In practical terms, this means, for example, that someone who has a food addiction makes eating the subject of his meditation. He first imagines in his meditation, as vividly as possible, eating his favorite foods. After doing this for a while, he imagines eating all the food he has ever seen. Then comes the turn of eating all plants, then eating all animals, then all people, then all objects, and finally all gods.

Because of his gluttony this meditation is quite easy for the person concerned and he reaches on the one hand a high concentration and ideally also one-pointedness and on the other hand also the experience of the unity of all things – everything is in his belly …

Similarly, the greed for power of a robber can be used as a motivational basis and also the desire of a person to always play music.

The robber was advised by the Mahasidda Tilopa to walk one-pointedly around a Buddhist stupa for seven days, by which he attained perfect one-pointedness and also the ability to do miracles (extraordinary magic) – but at the same time he also lost all interest in worldly power …

Another Mahasiddha recommended to a music-obsessed king to focus completely on the silence behind all sounds while playing his music. By doing so, this musician both realized the oneness of all things and attained single-mindedness.

Such "tricks" are found in the life stories of the Mahasiddhis in very large numbers. The most famous of these "tricks" is probably the Tibetan Tummo meditation (Tummo = Kundalini). The lamas have to practice Kundalini meditation until they are able to dip their clothes in water three times in the course of one night in the freezing winter and then dry them on their bodies by their meditation. The freezing temperatures are a guarantee that the motivation of the lamas is extremely high during this ordeal – causing them to become one-pointed and thus reach the state of ecstasy. From there it is not far to Da'ath magic …

IV 5. b)   Horoscope

If one is to become familiar with oneself, it is helpful to know oneself. How this is achieved is, of course, ultimately irrelevant. However, the horoscope is a good tool for this – it shows one's motivations, one's abilities, one's desires and one's style.

Consequently, if one has difficulty in becoming one-pointed, it might be helpful to study one's own horoscope in order to understand oneself better.

IV 5. c)   Hymn to oneself

When one has achieved a greater understanding of oneself, this should not remain a mere concept, but should become a basic self-affirming attitude. A possible tool to achieve this is the hymn to oneself.

For this hymn, one first collects statements about oneself, where one can say that they are definitely true. If you find this difficult, start with the simplest statements like "I am a human being" and "I am a man (or a woman)." Then you can add your name, your preferences, your abilities, etc.

The important point about this is merely that they are really true. They don't have to be something you would write in an application either, but also such things as "I'm an oddball." or "I'm a slowpoke." or "I'm constantly making new decisions."

You can also include important experiences you've had – no matter what they were. If it's an important memory, it belongs in the hymn.

If one knows one's own power animal, power plant and power stone, these naturally also belong in this hymn. The same applies to one's own soul and one's own patron deity.

All these statements should begin with "I am ...", "I do ...", "I have ..." etc. – after all it is a hymn to oneself.

These sentences can then be sorted thematically and thus gradually become the stanzas of a hymn. Verse meter, rhymes and the like are not necessary – if they arise in places by themselves, of course nothing speaks against it.

Of course, this hymn is never really finished, but can always be supplemented or rewritten.

If you have written a first version, you should read it aloud once and see how it feels. The good feelings about it should just be enjoyed and the unpleasant feelings should be looked at more closely – there is still potential there for correcting the words or for self-healing.

Finally, one should recite this hymn to a friend. Such a "lyrical self-expression" in front of a witness has a completely different effect than if one were to perform the hymn alone.

IV 5. d)   Uninhibitedness

Now that one has achieved a first taste of unity and a deeper understanding of oneself and has put this into a hymn, one can begin to let what one has found within oneself radiate.

The source of this radiance is ultimately one's own soul – the radiance itself is located primarily in the solar plexus and the throat chakra, as these are the two chakras that contain the unhindered self-expression in the healed state. In order to allow the identity in the heart chakra, that is, one's soul to radiate in these two chakras, it is necessary that the wish tree minor chakra at the bottom of the sternum and the thymus minor chakra at the top of the sternum are open.

When this is the case, one affirms what one is and then expresses it in the solar plexus by one's actions and in the throat chakra by one's attitude toward others. When these two minor chakras are partially closed by fears, addictions, pain, misconceptions, traumas, and the like, it is almost impossible to achieve radiance. So, in order to achieve uninhibited radiance, it is sometimes necessary to dissolve one or another old imprint of one's psyche beforehand.

Uninhibitedness has self-discovery and self-fidelity as its basis, by which one then lives completely out of one's own soul. The plant of non-restraint thrives best in the soil of self-love.

Inhibitionlessness is ultimately always an uninhibited self-expression. One is unin-hibitedly exactly what one is. One does what one wants. One wants intensely. One radiates at the maximum.

One does everything 100%. Thus telepathy becomes astral travel; thus telekinesis becomes a miracle; thus one reaches perfect self-expression.

Unrestrained self-expression means that one lives the essential with the greatest possible intensity.

IV 5. e)   Being in the Here and Now

An often mentioned aspect of single-mindedness and uninhibited self-expression is being present in the here and now. This does not at all mean blindness to everything that lies spatially and temporally around the moment, but merely the realization that only the moment is real, that one lives only where one is at the moment. Ideally, one always remains anchored in the point of the moment out of awareness of the whole.

Resting in the here and now also does not mean that one no longer thinks or has any concepts or worldview, but only that one's presence in the here and now always remains the pivotal point. Probably the Mahasiddha Maitripa formulated this attitude most vividly: "relaxing into the here and now."

In Tibetan Buddhism, this posture is a component of the mandala of the five Dhyani Buddhas, which represent the Buddha's biography:

> - This biography mandala begins in the west with <u>Buddha Amitabha</u>. He has his hands in his lap, contemplating himself and the world to understand its nature. This Buddha uses boundless serenity to recognize the world – he looks away from nothing, he makes nothing bigger or smaller than it is, and he sees things as they are.

> - When Buddha Amitabha has realized that the world is a unity at its root, he becomes the fearless <u>Buddha Amogasiddhi</u> sitting in the north of the mandala. He has attained the state of detachment, having realized the oneness of which he himself is also an expression. At the same time, he has also arrived fully in the here and now, as he sees unity behind everything and experiences it in every moment. This Buddha raises his left hand with the palm facing forward in a protective gesture in front of him.

- Since Buddha Amogasiddhi has attained fearless resting in the oneness underlying all multiplicity, he realizes that he will be happiest when all beings are happy. Thus, he becomes <u>Buddha Akshobhya</u>, seated in the east of the mandala. He is the boundless compassion with all beings that necessarily arises from the realization of the oneness of all things – his compassion is just his extended egoism. His gesture is touching the earth with the tip of his right middle finger – the gesture of invoking the earth as a witness to his realization and determination to help all beings achieve enlightenment.

- In order to become as happy as possible, Buddha Akshobhya must ultimately make all people happy, i.e. enlightened. This impulse then manifests as a boundless love for all beings, making him <u>Buddha Vairocana</u>, seated in the center of the mandala. His gesture is to turn the wheel of teaching in front of his heart chakra.

- First, Buddha Vairocana gives the teaching, that is, the explanation of his view and methods, to all who ask him for advice and help. After that, Buddha Vairocana also gives the transmission of power to those seeking advice, i.e. he takes them into his state of consciousness, by which they can already experience what they are trying to achieve with the help of Buddha. Thus Buddha Vairocana becomes <u>Buddha Ratnasambhava</u> sitting in the south of the mandala. Since this help is not work for Buddha, but the perfect self-expression resulting from his realization of the unity of all multiplicity and the continuum of all beings, a boundless joy arises from his living for the enlightenment of others.

Now, one does not have to become a Buddhist by any means in order to enter Da'ath consciousness and then to be able to perform Da'ath magic, but one can see some characteristics of the limitless state of Da'ath by the help of this Buddha mandala. Not everyone who attains Da'ath has a Buddhist worldview, but the individual elements can usually be found in slightly modified forms and in different combinations.

IV 5. f) <u>Letting go</u>

If one wants to move from the delimited state of consciousness to the delimitationless state of consciousness, one must logically give up one's limitations. This is only possible if one no longer defines oneself by one's boundaries but by one's quality – otherwise one would lose one's identity and panic when dissolving one's boundaries.

For this dissolving of the borders the courage is necessary to jump into the bottomless abyss, thus a letting go of any external support. This does not mean that afterwards one finds oneself in an endless free fall and in endless panic – even if the first encounter with the boundaryless state can be quite unsettling.

When one has found one's hold in oneself, i.e. no longer by one's boundaries, but in one's center, i.e. in one's own quality, the boundaryless state is a single pleasure … Buddha's "boundless joy". To reach this resting in one's own quality, the recognition of one's own soul is the greatest possible help – without this recognition it might be difficult to reach Da'ath in a relaxed way.

The unrestrained self-expression is the basis for the radiance that fills one from within and makes one's own identity so certain that one no longer needs delimitation.

On the one hand, one is completely focused on expressing and realizing what one is in one's innermost being, but on the other hand, one is completely independent of whether and how one can finally attain one's own self-expression. One strives for one's goals with all one's might, but is not dependent on their attainment for one's well-being. Fulfillment lies in self-fidelity, in one's own radiance … the attainment of one's goals is by no means uninteresting, but it always remains secondary.

Thus, the person acts single-mindedly and in perfect harmony with himself, being connected with everything and practicing Da'ath magic now and then. At the same time, however, he rests in himself and in the unity of the world and experiences what he is doing as a dance and simply makes the steps that just fit and enjoys the dance.

This results in an apparent paradox of being completely connected and engaged and at the same time completely independent and serene. Such apparent opposites can be found in many people who have reached this state.

IV 5. g) Anchoring

In addition to letting go, there is also an anchoring: resting in one's own patron deity, that is, in the source from which one's own soul has emerged. When one has found this deity, one does not have to do anything special in order for it to become one's own support and point of orientation – instead, one will notice that one's life proceeds according to the myths of this deity.

Then, when one realizes that one's soul has the qualities of this deity, and that one's psyche is in the most pleasant state when it lives according to these qualities, one comes into harmony with this deity without doing much.

Deities have a clear character, but no demarcation – they are therefore the natural anchor point for an identity that rests in its own quality and no longer needs any demarcation.

IV 5. h) Fullness

By letting go of demarcations and anchoring oneself in one's own protective deity, one gains a contact with the whole world in which one's own being is expressed. This creates a great abundance in one's life.

This does not necessarily mean wealth or the like, but a great abundance of the things that correspond to one's own patron deity, one's own soul and thus one's own psyche – a fulfilled life is created.

A preliminary stage to this fullness is the willingness to look at everything that one is and that one carries within oneself. By this, one finally sees oneself as one is, can accept and heal everything within oneself, and thus becomes one – self-fidelity has emerged.

Since the outside reflects the inside, by self-exploration and the dissolution of one's own fears, addictions and misconceptions, one can reach a state in which one is inwardly whole and in which consequently the outer state is also whole – after all, the outside reflects the inside.

Basically, everyone knows this reflection: fear evokes what it fears – love makes flourish what it loves.

If you want, you can also start at the fullness to reach Da'ath. To do this, one first builds up the mandala of the four elements plus the quintessence (light) – possibly with the help of the Lesser Pentagram Ritual.

Then one turns to the four archangels Raphael, Michael, Gabriel and Auriel one after the other and asks them for abundance in one's own life. Then one looks at what one receives from the archangels of air, fire, water and earth – what one can see in the ritual or meditation, and also what one subsequently experiences in one's own life.

Also this request for abundance to the archangels is an opening oneself to the boundless state of Da'ath: the archangels are in Da'ath and also their gifts are Da'ath gifts and consequently boundless gifts and therefore abundance. The intensity of the effect of this ritual or meditation depends on the intensity of the request for abundance of air, fire, water and earth as well as on the size of one's willingness to accept these gifts.

It may be helpful in this ritual to imagine one's own patron deity in the center of the mandala or to call this deity to the center – then it becomes the quintessence of abundance.

IV 5. i)   Let it happen

There is one more point, which at first is very similar to letting go, but which is something else. In some cases, the extraordinary magic is not directly intended, but the person simply does something out of a situation because it seems right to him and without suspecting that he is thereby working a "miracle". This is e.g. the case with some materializations, if they occur spontaneously, but fit entirely into the situation (in which at least one person is completely one-pointed).

Closely related to this phenomenon is the aspect of extraordinary magic that it is never used to "show off". There are cases when such magic is demonstrated to others, but even there it is used for the enrichment of others. This does not mean that one cannot perform extraordinary magic for oneself (Jesus could have rented a ship on the Sea of Galilee), but it is always connected to one's own truth and does not emanate from parts of the psyche that have been distorted by fears or addictions.

Often the extraordinary magic also simply arises out of the situation and is unplanned – it is a spontaneous act resp. event.

It does not seem to occur that someone performs a miracle for the sake of it. All cases of extraordinary magic have a direct motivation for miracles – and if the reason is merely to show in a court case that one is not an impostor (as some mahasiddhis have done).

In many cases it is described that the magicians do not perform their extraordinary magic out of themselves, but let it happen through them. As source of the miracles they experience God, a deity, their own patron deity or a similar "superior being" or just the "flow of the life force".

Finally, it is noticeable that there seem to be no instructions for extraordinary magic, no ritual, no rules, no fixed form – one simply does it. So extraordinary magic is not a craft where you learn step by step how to do it. Instead, extraordinary magic has as its foundation a certain state of consciousness from which the miracles are possible. So it is a matter of achieving that state of consciousness: Da'ath, the continuum, the lack of boundaries, the fully conscious collective subconsciousness, the consciousness of the gods …

IV 5. j)   Women and men

It is striking how few miracles are reported about women. In India there are women who performed miracles among the Mahasiddhis and also in Christianity among the saints, but they are clearly in the minority.

Of the 81 Mahasiddhis, only 5 are women (6%).

Of the 1384 Christian saints and blessed (all of whom either performed a miracle or are martyrs), only 232 are women (17%). If one counts only the saints and the blessed up to the time of the Reformation, one arrives at an even significantly smaller percentage of women.

This low percentage of women is certainly not due to a lower talent of women for extraordinary magic, but to the fact that in former times (and partly still today) they played a much smaller role in public life than men.

The proportion of women miracle workers in other cultures cannot be determined, since extraordinary magic is systematically performed only by the Mahasiddhis in India and in Christianity. In Islam, for example, miracles are spoken of only in small circles.

IV 6. One's own way

Every human being has his own biography, his own horoscope, his own cultural background, his own interests, talents, points of view, and so on. Therefore there are also the most different and partly completely opposite interpretations of extraordinary magic.

For example, there are the Christian saints who completely submit to God and let him act through themselves – but then there are also the Gnostics who strive to get rid of the "yoke of God's law" and consider their magic to be against God's will.

There are also those who see this kind of magic as the magical aspect of an ecological worldview (both of which are aspects of Da'ath).

Then there are some like Christ who always use their extraordinary magic for the benefit of all people, but also saints like Elijah who use their miracles to impose their worldview and kill the priests of other religions.

There are also many people who have occasionally performed extraordinary magic who have never given much thought to magic or worldviews or miracles.

It is obvious that the worldview is not the central element in extraordinary magic – although by almost everyone who has a clear worldview, their magic is seen as firmly connected to their worldview. Sometimes this worldview is even considered to be the foundation of extraordinary magic.

However, it seems more likely that extraordinary magic is possible for all people and depends only on whether or not one can achieve Da'ath consciousness.

V Summary

By extraordinary magic ("miracles", "Da'ath magic") the laws of nature are suspended. These include firewalks, materializations, matter transformations, spontaneous self-healings, healings by others, resurrections of the dead, and the like.

While doing this, one is completely attuned and "one just does it" – "it happens through one". Sometimes one also consciously "puts oneself into something bigger" – usually God or a deity.

While doing extraordinary magic, one has unlimited perception and unlimited ability to act – one is in Da'ath consciousness. Most people are in this state only on rare occasions and in special situations (if they ever reach it at all), but there is also the possibility of being in this consciousness most of the time.

Extraordinary magic is closely connected to lack of delimitation. Since without delimitations one also sees oneself completely, healing one's psyche and finding one's soul is a useful preparation for the ability to perform extraordinary magic. A good tool for this is the awakening of Kundalini. The goal is complete self-fidelity, "Do what you want.", unrestrained self-expression …

In order to become familiar with the lack of boundaries (continuum), dream journeys to deities, to Da'ath and especially to one's own patron deity are extremely beneficial. Also dream journeys to saints, magicians, yogis etc. to watch them performing their miracles are extremely helpful – one gets to know the "taste" of extraordinary magic. The central element is the invocation of one's own patron deity, that is, the most intense identification with it. The Da'ath ritual of transforming the four elements into each other can also be quite helpful.

Extraordinary magic always happens only in the here and now. Therefore, it is beneficial to practice being present in the moment.

In all this, it is always necessary to stay true to one's own style – otherwise one cannot be truly effective with one's own magic (and neither with everything else).

Extraordinary magic also exists without any preparation – but then it occurs only spontaneously in an extraordinary situation where extraordinary magic is needed to save oneself or others or the like. However, in order to be able to perform extraordinary magic on one's own initiative, Da'ath consciousness is necessary: Buddha's four boundless qualities of an enlightened one, the home in the continuum, the deity-consciousness – just Da'ath …

English Books by Harry Eilenstein

- Living Magic (261 p.)
- The Synthesis of Physics and Magic (192 p.)
- Telepathy for Beginners (60 p.)
- Telepathy for Advanced Learners (52 p.)
- Telekinesis for Beginners (56 p.)
- Life Force for Beginners (76 p.)
- Astral Projection for Beginners (60 p.)
- Meditation for Beginners (60 p.)
- Prophecy for Beginners (60 p.)
- Ritual Magic for Beginners (64 p.)
- Magic Chant for Beginners (108 p.)
- Invocations for Beginners (52 p.)
- Evocations for Beginners (62 p.)
- Auto-Movement for Beginners (60 p.)
- Elves for Beginners (56 p.)
- Hypnosis for Beginners (56 p.)
- Love Magic for Beginners (52 p.)
- Money Magic for Beginners (60 p.)
- Magic Objects for Beginners (64 p.)
- Shamanism for Beginners (52 p.)
- Chakra-Magic for Beginners (148 p.)
- Language of the Moon – for Beginners (128 p.)
- Self Knowledge for Beginners (60 p.)
- Da'ath-Magic for Beginners (64 p.)
- Astrology for Beginners (112 p.)
- Number Symbolism for Beginners (64 p.)
- Mandalas for Beginners (76 p.)
- Crop Circles for Beginners (344 p.)
- Feng Shui for Beginners (96 p.)

These books will be puplished soon:

- Kundalini for Beginners
- Magic Research for Beginners
- Symbolism of Numbers for Beginners
- Magic for Beginners – Anthology I
- Magic for Beginners – Anthology II
- Magic for Beginners – Anthology III
- Magic for Beginners – Anthology IV

Bücher von Harry Eilenstein

Religion allgemein
- Die sieben Schritte des Lebens (428 S.)
- Muttergöttin und Schamanen (168 S.)
- Göbekli Tepe (472 S.)
- Die Göttin von Göbekli Tepe (144 S.)
- Die Biographie des Teufels (144 S.)
- Totempfähle (440 S.)
- Christus (60 S.)
- Dakini (80 S.)
- Vajra (76 S.)

Ägypten
- Hathor und Re 1: Götter und Mythen im Alten Ägypten (432 S.)
- Hathor und Re 2: Die altägyptische Religion – Ursprünge, Kult und Magie (396 S.)
- Isis (508 S.)

Indogermanen
- Die Entwicklung der indogermanischen Religionen (700 S.)
- Wurzeln und Zweige der indogermanischen Religion (224 S.)

Germanen
- Die Götter der Germanen (87 Bände – siehe nächste Seite)
- Odin (300 S.)

Kelten
- Cernunnos (690 S.)
- Taliesin (228 S.)
- Der Kessel von Gundestrup (220 S.)
- Der Chiemsee-Kessel (76)

Psychologie
- Über die Freude (100 S.)
- Das Geheimnis des inneren Friedens (252 S.)
- Das Beziehungsmandala (52 S.)
- Gefühle und ihre Verwandlungen (404 S.)
- einsgerichtet (140 S.)
- Liebe und Eigenständigkeit (216 S.)
- Von innerer Fülle zu äußerem Gedeihen (52 S.)

Heilung
- Die Symbolik der Krankheiten (76 S.)

Kunst
- Herz des Tanzes – Tanz des Herzens (160 S.)

Drama
- König Athelstan (104 S.)

Bücher von Harry Eilenstein

„Magie für Anfänger"

- Telepathie für Anfänger (60 S.)
- Telepathie für Fortgeschrittene (52 S.)
- Telekinese für Anfänger (52 S.)
- Lebenskraft für Anfänger (60 S.)
- Meditation für Anfänger (56 S.)
- Kundalini für Anfänger (100 S.)
- Hypnose für Anfänger (56 S.)
- Auto-Movement für Anfänger (56 S.)
- Chakra-Magie für Anfänger (148 S.)
- Astralreisen für Anfänger (56 S.)
- Astrologie für Anfänger (120 S.)
- Ritual-Magie für Anfänger (56 S.)
- Mandalas für Anfänger (68 S.)
- Geldzauber für Anfänger (56 S.)
- Liebeszauber für Anfänger (52 S.)
- Invokationen für Anfänger (52 S.)
- Evokationen für Anfänger (60 S.)
- Elfen für Anfänger (56 S.)
- Magie-Forschung für Anfänger (140 S.)
- Selbsterkenntnis für Anfänger (52 S.)
- Zahlensymbolik für Anfänger (60 S.)
- Die Sprache des Mondes – für Anfänger (116 S.)
- Zaubergesänge für Anfänger (100 S.)
- Zukunftschau für Anfänger (60 S.)
- Schamanismus für Anfänger (52 S.)
- Magische Gegenstände für Anfänger (68 S.)
- Da'ath-Magie für Anfänger (64 S.)
- Kornkreise für Anfänger (348 S.)
- Feng Shui für Anfänger (96 S.)
- Magie für Anfänger – Sammelband I (696 S.)
- Magie für Anfänger – Sammelband II (664 S.)
- Magie für Anfänger – Sammelband III (580 S.)

„Traumreisen"

- Traumreisen zu Heilpflanzen (700 S.)

Magie

- Handbuch für Zauberlehrlinge (408 S.)
- Tarot (104 S.)
- Physik und Magie (184 S.)
- Die Synthese von Physik und Magie (200S.)
- Die Magie-Formel (156 S.)
- Krafttiere – Tiergöttinnen – Tiertänze (112 S.)
- Schwitzhütten (524 S.)
- Mythen und Magie der Harfe (116 S.)
- Magie heute – Berichte aus der Praxis (288 S.)

Meditation

- Der Lebenskraftkörper (230 S.)
- Die Chakren (100 S.)
- Das Chakren-System mit den Nebenchakren (296 S.)
- Organe und Chakren (64 S.)
- Die platonischen Körper in den Chakren (156 S.)
- Meditation (140 S.)
- Drachenfeuer (124 S.)
- Kundalini I (676 S.)
- Reinkarnation (156 S.)
- einsgerichtet (140 S.)

Astrologie

- Astrologie (496 S.)
- Photo-Astrologie (428 S.)
- Die astrologischen Aspekte (88 S.)
- Horoskop und Seele (120 S.)

Kabbala

- Kursus der praktischen Kabbala (150 S.)
- Eltern der Erde (450 S.)
- Blüten des Lebensbaumes:
  - Die Struktur des kabbalistischen Lebensbaumes (370 S.)
  - Der kabbalistische Lebensbaum als Forschungshilfsmittel (580 S.)
  - Der kabbalistische Lebensbaum als spirituelle Landkarte (520 S.)

Die Themen der 87 Bände der Reihe „Die Götter der Germanen"